Edwin Stanton

Secretary of War

Colonial Leaders

Lord Baltimore
English Politician and Colonist

Benjamin Banneker
American Mathematician and Astronomer

Sir William Berkeley
Governor of Virginia

William Bradford
Governor of Plymouth Colony

Jonathan Edwards
Colonial Religious Leader

Benjamin Franklin
American Statesman, Scientist, and Writer

Anne Hutchinson
Religious Leader

Cotton Mather
Author, Clergyman, and Scholar

Increase Mather
Clergyman and Scholar

James Oglethorpe
Humanitarian and Soldier

William Penn
Founder of Democracy

Sir Walter Raleigh
English Explorer and Author

Caesar Rodney
American Patriot

John Smith
English Explorer and Colonist

Miles Standish
Plymouth Colony Leader

Peter Stuyvesant
Dutch Military Leader

George Whitefield
Clergyman and Scholar

Roger Williams
Founder of Rhode Island

John Winthrop
Politician and Statesman

John Peter Zenger
Free Press Advocate

Revolutionary War Leaders

John Adams
Second U.S. President

Samuel Adams
Patriot

Ethan Allen
Revolutionary Hero

Benedict Arnold
Traitor to the Cause

John Burgoyne
British General

George Rogers Clark
American General

Lord Cornwallis
British General

Thomas Gage
British General

King George III
English Monarch

Nathanael Greene
Military Leader

Nathan Hale
Revolutionary Hero

Alexander Hamilton
First U.S. Secretary of the Treasury

John Hancock
President of the Continental Congress

Patrick Henry
American Statesman and Speaker

William Howe
British General

John Jay
First Chief Justice of the Supreme Court

Thomas Jefferson
Author of the Declaration of Independence

John Paul Jones
Father of the U.S. Navy

Thaddeus Kosciuszko
Polish General and Patriot

Lafayette
French Freedom Fighter

James Madison
Father of the Constitution

Francis Marion
The Swamp Fox

James Monroe
American Statesman

Thomas Paine
Political Writer

Molly Pitcher
Heroine

Paul Revere
American Patriot

Betsy Ross
American Patriot

Baron Von Steuben
American General

George Washington
First U.S. President

Anthony Wayne
American General

Famous Figures of the Civil War Era

John Brown
Abolitionist

Jefferson Davis
Confederate President

Frederick Douglass
Abolitionist and Author

Stephen A. Douglas
Champion of the Union

David Farragut
Union Admiral

Ulysses S. Grant
Military Leader and President

Stonewall Jackson
Confederate General

Joseph E. Johnston
Confederate General

Robert E. Lee
Confederate General

Abraham Lincoln
Civil War President

George Gordon Meade
Union General

George McClellan
Union General

William Henry Seward
Senator and Statesman

Philip Sheridan
Union General

William Sherman
Union General

Edwin Stanton
Secretary of War

Harriet Beecher Stowe
Author of Uncle Tom's Cabin

James Ewell Brown Stuart
Confederate General

Sojourner Truth
Abolitionist, Suffragist, and Preacher

Harriet Tubman
Leader of the Underground Railroad

Edwin Stanton

Secretary of War

Amy Allison

Arthur M. Schlesinger, jr.
Senior Consulting Editor

Chelsea House Publishers

Philadelphia

CHELSEA HOUSE PUBLISHERS
Editor-in-Chief Sally Cheney
Director of Production Kim Shinners
Production Manager Pamela Loos
Art Director Sara Davis
Production Editor Diann Grasse

Staff for *EDWIN STANTON*
Editor Sally Cheney
Associate Art Director Takeshi Takahashi
Series Design Keith Trego
Layout by D&G Limited, LLC

The Chelsea House World Wide Web address is
http://www.chelseahouse.com

First Printing
1 3 5 7 9 8 6 4 2

Library of Congress Cataloging-in-Publication Data

Allison, Amy, 1956-
    Edwin, Stanton, Union War Secretary / by Amy Allison.
       p. cm. — (Famous figures of the Civil War era)
    Includes bibliographical references (p.) and index.
    ISBN 0-7910-6420-4 (alk. paper) — ISBN 0-7910-6421-2 (pbk. :
    alk. paper)
       1. Stanton, Edwin McMasters, 1814-1869—Juvenile literature. 2.
    Statesmen—UnitedStates—Biography—Juvenile literature. 3. Cabi-
    net officers—United States—Biography—Juvenile literature. 4.
    United States. War Dept.—Biography— Juvenile literature. 5. Unit-
    ed States—Politics and government—1861-1865—Juvenile litera-
    ture. 6. United States—History—Civil War, 1861-1865—Juvenile
    Literature. [1. Stanton, Edwin McMasters, 1814-1869. 2. States-
    men. 3. United States—History—Civil War, 1861-1865.] I. Title. II.
    Series.

    E467.1.S8 A49 2001
    973.7'092—dc21
    [B]   2001028800

Contents

Men, women, and children were taken from Africa and brought to the United States. They were then sold to plantation owners in the South. Slaves worked for little or no money in the fields and homes of their owners, and they had no rights or freedoms. This arrangement benefited the plantation owners and was an important part of the Southern economy. Plantation owners could operate their farms with very few expenses.

"A Good Talker"

The Civil War threatened the United States with ruin. Intent on guarding against this threat was a man with a cool head and a steadfast heart. U.S. War Secretary Edwin McMasters Stanton directed the nation's resources into crushing the Confederate rebellion against the Union.

Edwin was born December 19, 1814, in Steubenville, Ohio. With his dark skin and eyes, the baby resembled his mother, Lucy. Edwin was five months old when his father, David, began studying to be a doctor.

Three years later, in May 1818, David Stanton was approved to practice medicine. He set up his practice in the Stantons' two-story home. Word soon spread of the young doctor's devotion to his patients.

He never made much money, but the Stanton's lived comfortably. Village doctors were sometimes paid in goods, not cash. In addition to Edwin, the family eventually included two daughters, Oella and Pamphilia, and a second son, Darwin.

David hoped that Edwin would be a doctor. He hung a human skeleton in the stable in back of the house for Edwin to study. Standing on barrels in the stable, Edwin held neighborhood children spellbound with lectures on the skeleton. One of these neighbors recalls Edwin as "a good talker, and very earnest."

Edwin was also a practical joker. He'd put a lighted candle inside the skull at night to scare passersby. He'd also horrify neighbors by dropping in on them with a snake coiled around his neck. Edwin and his brother, Darwin, hunted snakes, along with frogs and insects, for their father's collection. Dr. Stanton liked to impress visitors as well as patients with his display of some of nature's odder-looking creatures.

The mischief maker was a serious student, though. He especially loved to read. Edwin had started school at age six. At 10 years old he suffered his first asthma attack and grew even more attached to his books. Fits of wheezing and tortured breathing prevented him from joining in rough play with other boys.

Life dealt Edwin another blow on December 30, 1827, when his father died suddenly. Dr. Stanton had little to leave his family but the house they lived in. Lucy would have to find a way to support herself and her children. Adding groceries to her husband's stock of medicines, she opened a general store in the front room of the Stanton home.

To add to the family's support, 13-year-old Edwin quit school to serve as an **apprentice** to bookseller James Turnbull. Working as Turnbull's clerk, handyman, and errand boy, Edwin still found time to read. He sometimes became so absorbed in a book that he ignored customers.

Yet, Edwin's firsthand knowledge of the books in Turnbull's store served his employer well. He recommended books for customers to buy. He also organized a library, charging lenders 10 cents for the privilege of checking out books for a certain period of time.

Turnbull was pleased enough with his apprentice to allow him time off to keep up with his studies. But Edwin's ongoing bouts of asthma, along with his duties at the bookstore, kept him from the company of boys his age. Alone, on a rocky perch overlooking the Ohio River, Edwin spent hours daydreaming of wealth and success.

Convinced that the quickest road to success was education, Edwin decided to go to college. Daniel Collier, Lucy's lawyer and Edwin's guardian, loaned him the money to enroll. Turnbull, meanwhile, agreed to **suspend** the boy's apprenticeship.

At 16, dressed in a new suit, Edwin left Steubenville for the first time in his life. He excitedly boarded a stagecoach for Kenyon College. Located in Gambier, in central Ohio, Kenyon was known as "The Star in the West."

Wilderness still surrounded the campus. The ground was so often muddy, students scurried atop fences, single file, on their way to class. Rising at 5 A.M., they built their own fires and fetched their own water before breakfast. Also, students at Kenyon bent over plows in the school's fields as well as over their books.

Edwin's talent for winning others over to his side benefited him in school debates. A member of Kenyon's **debate** club, he argued the burning issues of the day with fellow students.

One such issue was slavery. Following his parents' example, Edwin spoke out against the ownership of one human being by another. David and Lucy Stanton assisted slaves escaping Virginia, whose hills were in view from their home across the Ohio River. Also, Dr. Stanton insisted on buying medicines locally to avoid supplying his practice with the products of slave labor.

A related hot topic of the day was states' rights. Many people, mostly in the South, were fiercely loyal to their own state. They insisted each state

A fugitive slave family is shown crossing the Rappahannock River in Virginia. Slaves could stop for help at safe houses in the Underground Railroad along the route to the North.

could decide which of the nation's laws they would obey and which they would not. But settlers of newer states in the West, like Ohio, were just as fiercely loyal to the national government, in Washington, D.C. After all, the national government, not the state, sold people their land and built their roads. In 1832 debates about slavery and states' rights grew so harsh at Kenyon that students from the South withdrew from the existing debate club to form their own. Later, Edwin recalled with a friend from Kenyon, "We fought the South together at Kenyon, and whipped."

The year 1832 brought defeat as well as victory to young Stanton. Lucy's store had failed, and Edwin was summoned back to Steuben-ville. His guardian, Daniel Collier, explained to Edwin that he'd have to earn a salary. That meant he must leave college. "I abandoned all hopes," he confessed to a classmate.

Edwin would again be working for Turnbull. But this time he'd be managing Turnbull's store in Colum-bus, the capital city of Ohio. By late September he was on a stagecoach bound for the capital. Jostling along the road, his spirits rebounded. He looked ahead to the opportunities the city promised a bright, ambitious young man like himself.

Kenyon College was started in 1824 by Philander Chase, the first Episcopal bishop of Ohio. The school was named after Lord Kenyon from England, one of the people who made a donation to help start the school. One night Edwin borrowed the bishop's horse to visit a young woman who lived in a log cabin in the forest near the school. The next morning Bishop Chase was furious when he found his horse tired out and spat-tered with mud. Edwin confessed and begged for forgiveness. The bishop was so moved by Edwin's pleas that he decided not to expel Edwin.

Salmon Chase was a lawyer from Cincinnati, Ohio. He defended runaway slaves in court cases. Edwin Stanton and Chase remained friends even though each belonged to different political parties.

Mr. Attorney Stanton

olumbus was enjoying a period of great growth when Edwin arrived there. The city's broad, paved sidewalks showed off its importance. Still, cows grazed on the Capitol grounds.

Edwin's new life in Columbus included a sweetheart. Edwin met Mary Lamson in church. Now he had a new reason to be ambitious. Edwin hoped to marry Mary and be able to support a family. He convinced Collier to allow him to study law in Collier's office back in Steubenville. Mary promised to wait for him.

The next two years Edwin dutifully helped prepare Collier's law cases. In August 1835 he passed the exam allowing him to practice law in Ohio. But, at 20, he was still too young to get a law license.

That didn't stop him from arguing cases in court, under Collier's watchful eye. In early fall, an opposing attorney demanded the underage Edwin be booted from the courtroom. Collier rose to his student's defense. Once Collier finished his defense, Edwin didn't wait for the judge to rule. He went right on with his argument.

Finally, in December 1835, Edwin turned 21. The state of Ohio granted Edwin his law license. He started the year 1836 in partnership with Chauncey Dewey, who had a prosperous practice in the city of Cadiz, which was the governing center of Harrison County. Dewey and Stanton took one side or the other of nearly every lawsuit brought in Harrison as well as in the surrounding counties.

Edwin became known around Cadiz as a tireless worker. He was known, too, as "Little Stanton." Edwin was shorter than most men, and stocky. He also wore a full beard and peered out at the world through thick glasses.

Edwin's appetite for work had its rewards. He was able to pay for medical school for his brother, Darwin. Also, he now made enough money to support a family. On December 31, 1836, he and Mary married in Columbus. Edwin remembered the 125-mile sleigh ride to the couple's new home in Cadiz as the "sweetest journey of all my life."

Mary and Edwin's brick house stood more than a mile from town. Edwin set up a furnace, which was then a new invention, in the basement. The front porch of the house looked out over a garden. Before heading off to his law office in the morning, Edwin happily hoed and raked the garden.

At age 22, Edwin's career was flourishing, and he was elected to represent Harrison

County in its law cases. He ran as a Democrat, upsetting the majority Whig party. During the campaign, he visited every home in the area with Mary by his side.

Edwin's association with Judge Benjamin Tappan encouraged his activity in politics. Tappan had served in the state senate and urged Edwin to join his Steubenville practice. Lawsuits were developing as fast as businesses along Steubenville's riverfront. Edwin agreed.

At first, Edwin stayed in Cadiz, where he still practiced law with Dewey. But then in 1838, Tappan won a U.S. Senate seat and moved to Washington, D.C. Tappan had asked his young partner to take over his widespread practice. Edwin and Mary moved from Cadiz and set up house near Edwin's Steubenville office.

Edwin deserved Tappan's trust in him. He argued forcefully for his clients in court. His dogged questioning upset many on the witness stand. Once he was so rude to a witness, the opposing attorney, Roderick Moodey, protested. Edwin ordered him to "quit whining."

"I don't think a whine is any worse than a bark," Moodey answered. He stressed the word *bark* as a swipe at Edwin's "bulldog" voice.

Edwin shot back: "There is a difference—dogs bark and puppies whine."

Before tensions exploded, the judge called for a break. But when Edwin returned to the courtroom, Moodey attacked him. Edwin's glasses and the papers he was carrying flew in all directions. Onlookers kept the two from a fist fight. The foes later became friends.

Edwin's determination to win earned him the most successful law practice in the area. Life at home was fulfilling, too. On March 11, 1841, Edwin and Mary's first child was born. The couple named the baby Lucy. But in August, little Lucy died. Mary gave birth to a son, Edwin Jr., the following year, on August 11.

Later that year, Edwin met Salmon Chase, a lawyer from Cincinnati, Ohio. Chase defended

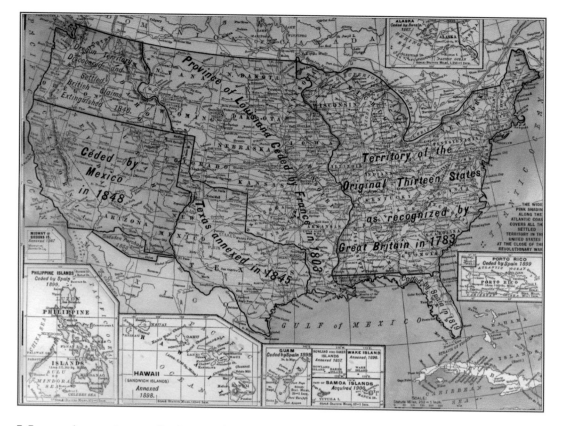

Many Americans believed in "Manifest Destiny." This was
the concept that the United States was destined to reach
from the Atlantic to the Pacific Ocean. This map shows
how the United States looked in the 1800s. As the country
grew, the question of whether or not new states would be
free states, or allow slavery, became important.

many runaway slaves in court. Edwin tried to

convince Chase that the Democratic Party

offered the best hope for the antislavery cause. Chase championed the newly formed Liberty Party. Neither man persuaded the other, but they stayed friends.

Rather than face the problem of slavery, many Americans preferred to consider the nation's "Manifest Destiny." They believed the United States was fated to reach from the Atlantic to the Pacific Ocean. Texas had won its independence from Mexico and sought to join the United States. The question loomed whether accepting Texas into the Union meant the spread of slavery. Edwin was among those alarmed over the question.

But events closer to home alarmed him more. Early in 1844, Mary fell ill, and on March 13, she died. Edwin was nearly insane with grief. He insisted Mary's burial clothes resemble her wedding gown, saying, "She is my bride and shall be dressed and buried like a bride." At night he'd search the house with a lamp, crying, "Where is Mary?"

No court could be held in Steubenville's Jefferson County while Edwin mourned for Mary. He was attached to every case. Demand for his services eventually brought him back to his senses. To further take his mind off his loss, he turned to politics.

President James Polk was talking about adding not only Texas, but also California to the United States. On May 12, 1846, a flare up between United States and Mexican border troops exploded into war. Patriotic feeling flooded America. Edwin wanted to support his country by signing up for the army, but his asthma kept him out of uniform.

Edwin's brother, Darwin, was also eager to sign up for the fight. But a fever struck him that affected his brain. In agony, the young doctor slit his own throat. Hearing of Darwin's death, Edwin ran wildly into the night in the woods surrounding Steubenville. Friends later found him and led him home.

New responsibilities shook him out of his sorrow. He invited Darwin's wife and three

General Winfield Scott and his men entered Mexico City in March and defeated Mexican troops in the last battle of the Mexican-American War. At the end of the war, the Treaty of Guadalupe Hidalgo set the southern boundary of Texas and gave New Mexico and California to the United States.

children to live with him and his son, Eddie. Edwin's mother and his sister Pamphilia had already moved into Edwin's home.

In a letter to Chase, Edwin wrote that recent events "have broken my spirits, crushed my hopes." Weighed down with memories as well as responsibilities, Edwin decided to start fresh in a new city. He chose Pittsburgh, a booming town in neighboring Pennsylvania.

Edwin devoted himself to his work. Work not only paid the bills. It also distracted him from his loneliness. Late at night, he'd take law books from his office to study them at home.

Politics now took a back seat in Edwin's life to his law practice. In 1848 the presidential candidates of the two main parties, the Democrats and Whigs, ignored the spread of slavery into new territories. Antislavery members of both parties joined Salmon Chase's Liberty organization to form the Free-Soil Party. The party's slogan was "Free soil, free speech, free labor, free men." Edwin supported the Free-Soilers—but only in private, when talking with friends. Public comment might cost him clients, just as his career was about to reach new heights.

President James Buchanan appointed Edwin as attorney general of the United States in 1860. Edwin took his post a few days before the Civil War started.

Attorney General

In 1847 construction started in Wheeling, Virginia, on one of the longest bridges ever built. Spanning the Ohio River, the bridge promised to make Wheeling a gateway to the nation's West. But the bridge wasn't tall enough for the huge smokestacks of steamer ships to clear. That left Pittsburgh, located beyond Wheeling, unreachable. With river traffic stopped at Wheeling, railroad lines would end there, too.

On August 16, 1849, Edwin appeared before U.S. Supreme Court Justice R. C. Grier on behalf of the state of Pennsylvania. He argued the bridge prevented the conduct of business between states. Grier agreed to hear the case.

To support his argument, Edwin traveled up and down the Ohio River. He busily gathered details about trade along the river.

Edwin supported his case with more than research. He also arranged for a steamer to advance under the bridge. A crowd watched as the steamer's 85-foot-tall smokestacks ripped away. This stunt helped Edwin win not only the case, but also publicity.

He was soon assisting in a case grabbing headlines nationwide. Back in 1831, Cyrus McCormick built a machine for harvesting grain that made him rich. Competitors jumped at the chance to produce similar machines. In 1854, McCormick sued a competitor, the John H. Manny Company, in the courts of Chicago, Illinois. Manny hired top attorneys George Harding and Peter Watson to defend him. They asked Edwin to join their legal team.

Harding and Watson also added a local Illinois lawyer, Abraham Lincoln, to the team.

When the case moved to Ohio, Lincoln tagged along. One day Edwin and Harding noticed the tall, gangly fellow on the steps of their hotel. They snubbed Lincoln's offer to go to the courthouse together and hurried off without him.

Edwin's detailed research and brilliant summation of the defense helped Manny win the case. McCormick challenged the ruling all the way to the Supreme Court in Washington, D.C. Early in 1858, Stanton argued the case, again successfully, before the country's highest court.

By then, Edwin had moved to Washington. The promise of more Supreme Court cases convinced Edwin to make the move. Joining him in Washington was his new wife, Ellen. Sixteen years younger than Edwin, Ellen Hutchison came from a well-known Pittsburgh family. The couple had been married at Ellen's home on June 25, 1856.

When James Buchanan became president in 1856, he named Jeremiah Black his **attorney general**. Black had struck up a friendship with Edwin in Pennsylvania. Now, as the country's most powerful lawyer, Black favored his friend with important government cases.

One such case resulted from the addition of California to the United States following a treaty with Mexico in 1848. The United States agreed to honor Mexican **land grants**, and land claims sprung up all over the state. The most ambitious claim, including much of San Francisco, was made by José Limantour. An employee of Limantour, Auguste Jouan, wrote to Black, hinting of wrongdoing in Limantour's claim. Black decided to fight the claim in court. In spring 1857 he asked Edwin to represent the U.S. government against Limantour in California.

Edwin took time answering. Ellen was slowly regaining strength after giving birth to a daughter on May 9, 1857. Finally, in October, Edwin accepted the job. Ellen would stay behind in Washington with their daughter, Eleanor.

In February 1858, Edwin started his ocean journey west. He devoted time on the trip to studying Spanish because papers he would have to examine in California would be written in that language. On March 19 his ship sailed into San Francisco harbor.

Edwin immediately began gathering papers on land grants under Mexican rule. Official papers were scattered far and wide after that rule collapsed in California. Only from a thorough review of records could he prove Limantour's dishonesty. As evidence against their client piled up, Limantour's lawyers abandoned him, and his claim was thrown out of court.

In February 1859, Edwin returned to Washington in triumph. Black turned to Edwin for help so often now, many considered Stanton an unofficial assistant attorney general.

Despite his success, Edwin felt discouraged. His country's future looked grim. Reflecting the deep divisions in America over slavery and states' rights, the 1860 presidential race split four ways. One candidate represented the newly formed Constitutional Union Party. Two opposing candidates ran under the Democratic Party banner. The Republicans, formerly Free-Soilers, passed over their front runners to nominate the almost unknown Abraham Lincoln.

Edwin suspected the Democratic Party divide would lead to Lincoln's win. He urged his Republican brother-in-law, Christopher Wolcott, to come to Washington as an early office-seeker. "The election of Lincoln," he wrote Wolcott, "is as certain as any future event can be." Edwin guessed right.

But until **Inauguration** Day, March 3, James Buchanan was still president. He hoped to calm the Southern states, which were enraged over Lincoln's election. They threatened to leave the Union, despite Buchanan's soothing speeches.

On December 20, 1860, the U.S. flag was lowered in South Carolina, and the state's own flag was raised in its place. The people of South Carolina declared themselves an independent nation.

That same day, Edwin read in the newspaper that he'd been appointed attorney general.

Buchanan's secretary of state had **resigned** and been replaced with Black. Black urged Buchanan to appoint Edwin to his old post.

Edwin accepted reluctantly. Public office paid far less than private practice. On the other hand, serving as attorney general would boost his legal reputation. Patriotic feelings also moved Edwin to serve. He wrote to a friend, "After much hesitation and serious reflection, I resolved to accept the post . . . in the hope of doing something to save this Government."

The day Edwin started his job, December 27, news came from Major Robert Anderson in South Carolina. Anderson commanded the Union defenses of Charleston harbor. The day before, he had moved his troops from Fort Moultrie to Fort Sumter, a more secure stronghold. South Carolina viewed the move with suspicion. On December 28, South Carolina's governor ordered Fort Moultrie seized, along with its store of weapons.

Buchanan called an emergency meeting of his cabinet. Some cabinet members demanded that Anderson leave Fort Sumter. But Edwin argued that Fort Sumter was government property. If Buchanan surrendered it, he would be guilty of treason. "We had high words," Edwin said, "and had almost come to blows."

Meeting again the next evening with cabinet members, Buchanan presented his reply to representatives from South Carolina. The representatives were in Washington to **negotiate** a treaty. Edwin argued, "These gentlemen . . . are lawbreakers, traitors. They should be arrested. You cannot negotiate with them."

On December 30, both Edwin and Black threatened to resign if Buchanan ordered Anderson from Fort Sumter. Eager to avoid further breakup of his cabinet, Buchanan agreed to toughen his reply. He responded to South Carolina's demand that U.S. forces leave Charleston harbor, "This I cannot do; this I will not do."

The South Carolinians were angry and left Washington. One of them claimed Buchanan

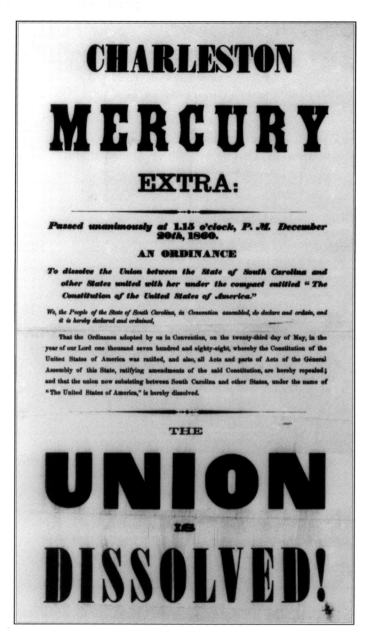

This broadside announces South
Carolina's secession from the Union.

"Young, expert riders, willing to face death daily," read ads for the Pony Express. Created in 1860, the Pony Express was a high-speed coast-to-coast mail service. Its riders faced death as they traveled through unfriendly Native American territory. "Buffalo Bill" Cody once rode 322 miles without stopping when his relief rider fell victim to Native American warriors. One Pony Express horse delivered the mail itself when its rider was killed. In 1861 the Pony Express ended. A cheaper, faster, and safer way to send messages had been introduced: a **telegraph**.

would have surrendered Fort Sumter if not "terrorized by Mr. Stanton."

In January 1861, Mississippi, Florida, and Alabama also **seceded** from the Union. Early in February, representatives of the seceding states proclaimed themselves the Confederate States of America. They elected Jefferson Davis president and set the date, February 18, for Davis's inauguration.

Edwin's gloom failed to lift at Lincoln's inauguration the following month. What he knew of the new president didn't inspire confidence.

Pictured here is Pony Express rider Frank. E. Webner, one of the brave men who delivered mail across the country.

Fort Sumter was a Union outpost in Charleston Harbor, off the coast of South Carolina. The fort was attacked by Confederate forces on April 12, 1861. This attack marked the start of the Civil War.

4

War Chief

Tension hung over Washington, D.C., following Lincoln's inauguration. "Not one of the cabinet or principal officers has taken a house or brought his family here," Edwin wrote to Buchanan. "They all act as though they meant to be ready to 'cut and run' at a minute's notice." The nation's capital, in fact, stood at the border of Confederate territory. The Confederates had set up their own capital at Richmond, Virginia, almost within cannon shot of Washington.

On April 12, 1861, Confederates fired on Fort Sumter. The war had begun.

On July 4, Independence Day, President Lincoln called on volunteers to take up arms to defend the

Union. Two days later, Virginia seceded. Arkansas and Tennessee quickly followed.

Soon afterward, Confederate forces tore up railroad tracks and telegraph wires north and west of Washington. The capital was temporarily cut off from the rest of the North. Once mail could again be exchanged, Edwin wrote a letter to his son, Eddie, then a student at Kenyon College. "Last week there was a great panic . . . and there seemed to be danger of a famine," Edwin said in his letter. He counted about 20,000 troops in Washington, some camped across from the Stanton home.

On July 21, 1861, Union troops began marching southward, into Virginia. "On to Richmond!" shouted headlines across the North. Confidence ran high that the Confederacy would soon fall. Hundreds of people followed the army for what they believed would be their only chance to see fighting. That evening the terrified crowd was racing back to Washington.

That meeting between the Confederate and Union soldiers at the First Battle of Bull Run ended with the Northern army retreating in panic. The North now realized that a hard fight lay ahead.

At that time the War Department, under war secretary Simon Cameron, was completely disorganized. Salmon Chase, Lincoln's treasury secretary, suggested his old friend Edwin as a replacement. George Harding, an attorney in the McCormick case, reintroduced Lincoln and Stanton. Harding later admitted his nervousness over memories of Edwin's snub of Lincoln. "The meeting was brief and friendly," he reported with relief.

On January 14, 1862, Lincoln appointed Edwin his secretary of war. Attorney General Edward Bates judged the new war secretary "a man of mind and action." John G. Nicolay, one of Lincoln's secretaries, looked forward to "great reforms in the War Department."

Edwin started his reforms with the War Department building. He added two stories, to more than double the office space. He could then bring under one roof the many department workers scattered about Washington. In the rebuilt War Office, Edwin set up the army's telegraph in an office next to his. With telegraph operators nearby, he could direct troops and equipment to battlefields with little delay.

Additionally, Edwin's tight control over the telegraph kept Union army movements secret. Military messages were sent in codes known only to Union telegraph operators.

The war secretary combated dangers from within as well as outside the North. Many Northerners sympathized with the Southerners. Edwin organized a secret police force called the "National Detectives" to unmask disloyalty. Even before Edwin took office, hundreds of people were in prison for acting suspiciously. President Lincoln used his emergency war powers to order them jailed indefinitely without charge. The War Office handled the arrests and then became the target of protests.

The angry citizens didn't surprise Edwin. "No public man in times like these can fail to have both his words and acts misunderstood," he wrote to a friend.

Grumbling against Edwin also came from army suppliers eager to profit from the country's crisis. To limit dishonesty, the war secretary insisted on open, competitive bidding for government **contracts**. In addition, suppliers failing to meet standards detailed in contracts faced arrest. Edwin was determined that Union soldiers wear shoes whose soles would not wear away after half a day's march.

Also, Edwin forbid buying from other countries any supplies that were available in the United States. This not only stopped the flow overseas of gold the government needed to pay for the war, it also encouraged the nation's industrial development.

Edwin's dedication and drive impressed the president. Edwin rarely returned home from the War Office before 10 P.M. He was back the next morning at nine. Tuesday through Thursday he and his staff worked on nothing but managing

Edwin served the Union as secretary of war under Lincoln. Edwin protected the Northern soldiers by making sure that they always had enough, food, clothing, and supplies throughout the war.

soldiers and supplies on the field. Saturdays were scheduled for meetings with members of Congress. Edwin was smart to develop relationships with Congressmen. Bills, appointments, and requests for money from the War Department moved quickly through Congressional committees.

On Monday mornings the War Office opened its doors to the public. Office seekers, grieving widows, dismissed officers, wounded soldiers, deserters, and army suppliers crowded a room next to Edwin's office on the second floor. There, Edwin sat behind a chest-high desk. One by one, people approached with their requests.

Edwin dealt out decisions swiftly and firmly. He might tear up a contract and fling its pieces at the supplier who presented it. He even turned down his nephew's request for an army post. John Hay, Lincoln's secretary, said he'd rather "make a tour of a smallpox hospital" than to ask special favors of the war secretary.

Edwin allowed himself few pleasures. Three mornings a week, on his way to the War Office, he'd visit the city market. The sights and smells of the busy market reminded him of the country life he knew as a boy in Ohio. When the pressures of work were too great, he'd shut himself in his office and read a novel.

The pressures grew as the Union's Army of the Potomac, headquartered in Washington, failed to launch a major attack against the South. Treasury Secretary Chase warned that, without any military success to show for the expense of war, he could "grind out no more money."

General in Chief George McClellan commanded the Army of the Potomac. He only seemed interested in using his troops for drills and parades. "*This army has got to fight,*" Edwin declared. He feared the South was building up its defenses as McClellan stalled.

By contrast, the Union army was on the move in Tennessee. Troops under General Ulysses S. Grant captured Fort Henry on February 6. By February 17, Grant held Fort Donelson, too. In the War Office, Edwin led three cheers for Grant. The shouts, wrote a clerk,

The Union Army of the Potomac was headquartered in Washington, D. C., and commanded by General George McClellan at the beginning of the war. These troops joined with other Union forces and headed toward the Confederate capital of Virginia.

"shook the old walls, broke all the spiders' webs, and set the rats scampering."

In March, McClellan finally led the Army of the Potomac southward. Word had spread that the Confederates abandoned their position in

People in Richmond, Virginia, frowned on Elizabeth Van Lew's anti-slavery ideas and called her Crazy Bet. She began acting the part: talking to herself and dressing in rags. Unsuspecting guards let her bring books to Union prisoners of war. Before returning them to her, the prisoners underlined various words in the books. Van Lew translated the coded messages in these words. The messages traveled to the North, in hollowed-out eggs filling baskets of produce carried by Van Lew's servants. Thanks to Crazy Bet, reports reached Union generals directly from the prisoners being held in the Confederate capital.

Bull Run, just south of Washington. McClellan was surprised at the site to find no cannons. Instead he found logs that were painted black to resemble cannons.

The Cabinet met, and Edwin demanded the army fire McClellan. Supporting him, Attorney General Bates urged Lincoln to accept the power the Constitution gave him as commander in chief, and "command the commanders." That night the president ordered McClellan to step down as general in chief and lead only the Army of the Potomac. All army divisions would report directly to the secretary of war.

Edwin and the president, together, were now the commanding generals of the Union forces.

Confederate troops were led into battle by famous generals such as Robert E. Lee and "Stonewall" Jackson. These Southern soldiers from Louisiana posed for photographer J. W. Petty.

Organizer of Victory

Edwin used the Union's industrial power to help the war effort. With its impressive military might, the North felt confident of victory. This confidence led Edwin into a major blunder. On April 3, 1862, he closed down army **recruiting** offices from state to state. They would reopen on June 16, with the goal of building each army unit to full strength.

Edwin rightly saw the need to reform the recruiting system. Strengthening existing units rather than simply creating new ones would produce a more efficient army. But in the meantime, the loss of recruits hurt the Union cause. The public blamed the war secretary for McClellan's failure to win a swift victory.

The criticism came at a difficult time for Edwin. His son, James, not yet nine months old, died on July 8. Worn out from grief, Edwin considered resigning. But President Lincoln urged him to stay.

With victory escaping his grasp, Lincoln sought the help of a military expert. On July 11 he gave General Henry Halleck command of the army. Halleck had the nickname "Old Brains" because he'd written several books on warfare.

All eyes were on the Virginia campaign. On August 30 came news that Union General John Pope was under heavy fire from Confederate General Robert E. Lee at the Second Battle of Bull Run. Cannon shots could be heard in Washington, and the wind carried the smell of gunpowder. Halleck pleaded with McClellan to join the battle and save Pope's troops from a bloodbath. Judging Pope's situation hopeless, McClellan refused. He advised Halleck to concentrate on the defense of Washington.

In the capital, the secretary of war was "steaming about with vigor, under great pressure, issuing . . . orders to be executed 'at once' for the safety of the city," reported General M. C. Meigs. Among Edwin's orders was to bundle up important War Department papers, ready to be carried to safety. "[A]t first we all thought," said Meigs, "the capital was really going to be captured."

Instead, Lee turned his army toward Maryland. With a little persuading, that slaveholding state might join the Confederacy.

The Unions troops straggling back to Washington were deeply discouraged by their defeat at the Second Battle of Bull Run. Lincoln put all Union regiments in Virginia under McClellan's Army of the Potomac. McClellan was still the soldiers' favorite general. Cheering, they followed him after Lee.

The army moved slowly. Finally, on September 14, McClellan met Lee near Antietam

Creek. Two days later came reports the Union army had beaten the Confederates back to the Potomac River. Lincoln expected to hear that McClellan had smashed Lee's weakened forces. Instead news arrived that the general had allowed Lee to cross the Potomac to safety. "McClellan has the slows," Lincoln stated; however, he waited until November to remove the general from command.

Lincoln had a more important announcement to make. On September 22 he told his cabinet he would now issue his **Emancipation** Proclamation. This freed slaves in states in rebellion, beginning January 1, 1863. Lincoln first presented the idea to the cabinet in July. It was then decided to issue the proclamation following a military victory. The news would be more welcome if accompanied by "fife and drum and public spirit." Antietam supplied the long-awaited victory.

For some time, Edwin hoped to sign up African Americans for the army. Arming blacks

President Lincoln (center) meets with Union General George McClellan (facing Lincoln) on the battlefield at Antietam, Virginia. The Battle of Antieram was the bloodiest one-day battle of the war. McClellan allowed Lee's troops to retreat to safety, which led to McClellan being relieved of his command.

to kill whites would alarm too many people, he was told, so the ban on African Americans in the army remained. Now Edwin argued that military service followed logically from emancipation.

President Lincoln is shown reading the Emancipation Proclamation to members of his Cabinet in September 1862. The final proclamation was issued on January 1, 1863, and freed slaves in the Confederate states that were in rebellion.

Lincoln agreed. In his Emancipation Proclamation, he declared that African Americans "will be received into the armed service of the United States." Proving Edwin right, African Americans joined the army in large numbers.

The Union war machine constantly demanded soldiers. In March 3, 1863, Congress passed a bill enforcing a national **draft**. Edwin argued against the bill's allowing $300 payment for a substitute. He wanted men, not money, he said.

Many protested that rich people buying their way out of military service was unfair. Some even complained that poor whites were being forced to fight to free blacks, who would come north and take their jobs. When the draft offices opened in New York City on July 13, a riot broke out. Rioters smashed and burned the buildings housing the offices. They also unleashed their anger on African Americans. At least a dozen blacks were murdered. By July 15 the mob swarmed the city.

That night, troops sent by the War Department arrived. The next day, the troops and the city's police brought the mob under control. On August 19 the draft offices reopened. Edwin ordered a total of 10,000 armed men to guard them. There were no more riots.

Demand for soldiers continued. On September 22 an urgent call for **reinforcements** came to the War Office from General William Rose-crans in Tennessee. Earlier that month, the Union army had taken the city the Confederates valued as their entry to the West.

Edwin ordered a midnight cabinet meeting. He proposed sending Rosecrans 30,000 rein-forcements from the Army of the Potomac. The troops would reach Chattanooga, Tennessee, in five days, he said. The president and other cabi-net members sat stunned. The transfer would take at least 40 days, Halleck claimed. Finally, at 2:30 A.M., Lincoln agreed to send 20,000 troops.

The next day the presidents of the nation's two major railroads planned the fastest possible route for the reinforcements. Edwin had already persuaded the owners of U.S. railways to turn their trains and tracks over to the army when needed. The Civil War was the first great conflict wherein railroads played a part.

Forty-eight hours after Rosecrans's message reached the War Office, fresh troops were speed-ing toward Chattanooga. The trains carrying

**Shown here is a regiment of African-American sol-
diers in the Union Army. Edwin Stanton was in
favor of enlisting blacks, and many blacks signed up
to fight after the Emancipation Proclamation
declared that they "will be received into the armed
service of the United States."**

them stretched six miles long. Less than 10 days
after Edwin put his plan in action, Rosecrans had
his reinforcements. Stanton had managed the
fastest mass movement of troops yet in history.

Rosecrans held on—but just barely. Edwin
rushed to meet General Grant at Louisville,

Kentucky. There, the war secretary handed Grant an order from Lincoln. The order gave Grant command of all Union forces between the Allegheny Mountains and the Mississippi River. While Grant was in charge, the army retreated from Chattanooga.

On March 9, 1864, Grant was rewarded with command of the entire Union army. He planned an all-out attack on the South. He aimed to pursue Lee without mercy. At the same time, he ordered General William Tecumseh Sherman to lay waste to Georgia. This meant that Lee could no longer depend on the state's riches for supplies.

Edwin had urged a bold thrust against the enemy from the beginning. He now busied himself supporting Grant's plan with huge amounts of weapons, horses, mules, wagons, timber, and medical supplies.

On April 3, 1865, a 16-year-old telegraph operator was on duty to pass on news of Richmond's capture. Crowds complete with brass bands stopped at the homes of cabinet members, demanding speeches. During his speech, Edwin paused several times, overcome with emotion.

On April 9, 1865, a weary Edwin welcomed the news of Lee's surrender to Grant. The next day, he handed Lincoln his resignation. The president responded, "Stanton, you have been a good friend and a faithful public officer and it is not for you to say when you will be no longer needed here."

Edwin could not deny the wishes of the president. Lincoln had reawakened ideals from his youth. Now Edwin feared the defeated enemy might seek revenge on the Union by attacking Lincoln. Over the president's protests, Edwin increased the number of guards protecting him.

President Lincoln often attended the theater in the war's final days. Theatergoing offered him an escape from his many cares. He invited Grant, Edwin, and their wives to accompany him and Mrs. Lincoln to Ford's Theater on April 14. Both couples declined.

"**M**EN OF COLOR, TO ARMS! NOW OR NEVER!" headlined a recruitment poster urging African Americans to sign up for the Union army. The poster read, in part: "This is our Golden Moment. . . . We must now awake, arise, or be forever fallen. If we value Liberty, if we wish to be free in this land, if we love our country, if we love our families, our children, our homes, we must strike NOW while the Country calls . . . and show by our own right arms that we are worthy to be freemen."

That night, about 10 o'clock, a messenger burst in on the Stantons. He ranted that Secretary of State William Seward had been attacked. Pushing his way through the crowd at Seward's, Edwin entered the secretary of state's blood-spattered bedroom. A doctor hovered over Seward, treating his stab wounds. From Sergeant Louis Koerth, who was in the crowd, Edwin first heard that President Lincoln had been shot.

Fearing a far-reaching plot, Edwin ordered Koerth to set up guards at the homes of all cabinet members and the vice president. He then raced over to the Ford Theater. Lincoln had been carried to a home across from the theater. There Edwin found him laid out on a bed, unconscious.

Immediately, Edwin set about avenging the attack on the president. By 3 A.M., an order went out for the arrest of actor John Wilkes Booth. At 7:22 A.M., Lincoln died. Edwin murmured, "Now he belongs to the ages."

These ruins in Columbia, South Carolina, were typical of
the devastation in the South.

Defender of
the Union

No, you must keep the machinery moving," the new president, Andrew Johnson, told Edwin when the war secretary offered to resign. "We must retain the chief engineer, by all means."

The great war machine Edwin helped create had a new task. It had to bring stability to the war-torn South. Before self-government could begin again, order needed to be established. The task was unusual. Never before in American history had American soldiers served as an occupying force on American soil.

Lincoln had suggested a **Reconstruction** plan in 1863. It offered to pardon and restore most property, except slaves, to Confederates who swore to uphold the Constitution, the Union, and the Emancipation Proclamation. The pardon included the right to vote. Further, a Confederate state was allowed to form a government and adopt a constitution if 10 percent of the people who voted in the 1860 presidential election took an oath of loyalty to the United States. The plan still had to be shown to work.

Edwin, as the army's "chief engineer," dealt daily with the realities of Reconstruction. Reports convinced him that Southern whites refused to accept defeat. They were electing their old leaders, many still unpardoned, to positions of power.

Such officials enacted Black Codes. These barred African Americans from jury duty and allowed them to sue only other African Americans. They also dealt harsher punishments to blacks than whites for many crimes. Senator Charles Sumner called the Black Codes slavery under a new name.

In March 3, 1865, Congress created the Freedman's Bureau within the War Department. It protected the rights of Southern blacks. In the final weeks of 1865, Edwin ordered that cases involving African Americans be tried in military courts, overseen by the Freedman's Bureau. Edwin was convinced that only the presence of the army protected African Americans, as well as white Unionists, from injustice in the South.

But to Edwin's alarm, President Johnson pushed for limiting the army's power in Southern states. On April 2, 1866, Johnson proclaimed the rebellion ended and the Southern states admitted back into the Union. This immediately removed the South from military command. Edwin was outraged. He declared that only if Johnson could bring back to life "the 300,000 Union dead would the nation accept the proclamation."

Edwin and the army were caught in a struggle between the president and Congress over Reconstruction. The war secretary turned his support to Congress. Early in 1867, Congress passed a Reconstruction Act. It returned the South to military rule until "loyal" state governments could be established. Also, it extended voting rights to African Americans in the South. Edwin was the only cabinet member who spoke in favor of the Reconstruction Act.

Despite pressures to resign, Edwin held on. He felt responsible for preserving the Union's hard-won victories on the battlefield. Congress depended on the president to enforce the laws it passed on Reconstruction. Edwin feared that Johnson would not support Congress's actions. The need for Congress to pass two more Reconstruction Acts supported Edwin's fears.

Edwin, in fact, helped prepare the Third Reconstruction Act. It became law on July 19 and gave Congress complete control over the occupying army. Edwin was satisfied the president could no longer frustrate the army's role in repairing the United States.

Johnson plotted his revenge. On August 12, Edwin learned the president was suspending him from the War Office. In March, Congress had passed the **Tenure** of Office Act. It prevented the president from dismissing officials without the Senate's agreement. But when the Senate was not in session, the president could **suspend** an official, then report to the Senate once it reassembled. From August to December, members of Congress were away from Washington.

Edwin submitted to the suspension under protest. But to his relief, General Ulysses S. Grant would fill in for him at the War Department. He trusted Grant not to abandon the army to Johnson.

Finally, on January 13, 1868, a messenger from Congress arrived at Edwin's home. The Senate ordered Edwin to return to his job as war secretary. The next morning he rushed over to the War Office, but he never again attended a cabinet meeting.

The president hadn't given up on ridding himself of his stubborn war secretary. On February 21 he sent General Lorenzo Thomas to the

Civil War hero General Ulysses S. Grant was put in charge of the War Department after Edwin was removed from the post by President Andrew Johnson.

War Office with orders dismissing Edwin. Thomas would manage the War Department until Johnson could appoint a replacement. Edwin snapped at the general, "I don't know whether I shall obey your orders or not."

Edwin promised to "continue in possession" of the War Office "unless expelled by force." He'd sleep on the sofa as he often did during the war when awaiting news from the front. Grant stationed guards around the building to keep Edwin from being physically removed.

On the snowy afternoon of February 24, the House of Representatives **impeached** Johnson. They charged him with disobeying the Tenure of Office Act. For the first time in the nation's history, a president faced legal charges brought against him by Congress.

On March 1, Senators began hearing arguments in the trial against Johnson. The strain, along with increasing bouts of asthma, wrecked Edwin's health. The final blow came on May 26. The Senate failed to convict Johnson by a single vote. The same day, Edwin sent his letter of resignation to the White House.

In early June, Congress formally thanked Edwin for his wartime service. They also praised

On March 1, 1868, Senators began hearing arguments in the impeachment trial of President Johnson. The president had disobeyed the Tenure of Office act when he tried to dismiss Edwin from office without the Senate's approval.

his efforts after the war to enforce laws "provided by Congress for the restoration of a real and permanent peace."

Edwin had always been highly regarded by his peers. Not long after Lincoln's funeral, some words of John Hay had filled Edwin with pride. Hay said: "It is already known, as well as the readers of history a hundred years hence will know, that no honest man has cause to quarrel with you, that your hands have been clean and year heart steady every hour of this fight, and that if any human names are to have the glory of this victory, it belongs to you among the very few who stood by the side of [Lincoln]."

President Lincoln had once said about Edwin, "He is the rock on the beach of our national ocean against which the breakers dash and roar. . . . He fights back the angry waters and prevents them from undermining and overwhelming the land." In other words: In defense of the nation, Edwin Stanton never backed down.

In 1789, Congress created the Department of War to manage the nation's military might. Heading the department was the secretary of war, a member of the president's cabinet. Then in 1798, Congress set up a separate Department of the Navy, with its own cabinet secretary. After World War II ended in 1945, the armed forces again united under a single command. The hope was for greater cooperation among the military's three branches, which now included an air force. In 1949 the combined forces of the army, navy, and air force became known as the Department of Defense, with the secretary of defense as its leader.

But praise could not pay Edwin's stack of bills. Although physically weak, he labored to rebuild his law practice. Then, in early December 1869, Edwin received a heartening message from the White House. Grant, now president, wished to appoint him to the U.S. Supreme Court. In a note thanking Grant, Edwin wrote: "It is the only public office I ever desired and I accept it with great pleasure."

On December 22, a fit of severe coughing weakened Edwin. The following day, the coughing grew even more violent. At midnight, Edwin lost consciousness. In the early morning hours of December 24, he died. He hadn't yet taken his seat on the Supreme Court.

The day of Edwin's funeral, December 27, was gray with rain. At President Grant's command, guns fired at army camps around the country to salute the former war secretary.

GLOSSARY

apprentice–someone serving another for a certain period to learn a skill or job.

attorney general–the chief lawyer of a nation or state; advises the government on legal matters.

contract–an agreement to supply goods or services at a set price; signers are legally required to fulfill the agreement.

debate–to discuss a topic by presenting opposing arguments.

draft–a system of selecting individuals for required military service.

emancipation–freeing from slavery or imprisonment.

impeach–to charge a public official with a crime.

inauguration–a ceremony swearing an official into office.

land grants–gifts of land made by the government.

negotiate–to settle a disagreement or other matter.

Reconstruction–the process of bringing the seceded states back into the Union after the Civil War.

recruiting–adding members to the armed forces.

reinforcements–additional troops.

resign–give up an office or position.

secede–to break away from a political group or nation.

suspend–remove temporarily from an office or position.

telegraph–a system for sending messages over long distances in coded signals.

tenure–protection from dismissal without a formal review.

CHRONOLOGY

1814	Edwin is born in Steubenville, Ohio, to Dr. David and Lucy Stanton, on December 19.
1831	Attends Kenyon College.
1835	Licensed to practice law in Ohio.
1835	Marries Mary Lamson on December 31.
1841	Daughter Lucy born in March and dies in August.
1842	Son Edwin Jr. born on August 11.
1844	Breaks down when Mary dies.
1849	Argues Wheeling bridge case before the U.S. Supreme Court.
1854	Joins legal team in the high-stakes McCormick reaper case filed in Chicago; meets Abraham Lincoln, a local Illinois lawyer assisting the team.
1856	Marries Ellen Hutchison on June 25 and moves to Washington, D.C.
1857	Assists Attorney General Black in land grant case; daughter Eleanor born on May 9.
1860	Appointed Attorney General under President James Buchanan.
1862	Appointed President Abraham Lincoln's secretary of war.
1863	Manages the fastest mass movement of troops yet in history, sending Union reinforcements by train to Chattanooga.
1868	Dismissal from the War Department leads to President Andrew Johnson's impeachment; resigns when the Senate fails to convict Johnson.
1869	Appointed Supreme Court justice by President Ulysses S. Grant; dies, on December 24, before taking his seat on the Court.

CIVIL WAR TIME LINE ===

1860   Abraham Lincoln is elected president of the United States on November 6. During the next few months, Southern states begin to break away from the Union.

1861   On April 12, the Confederates attack Fort Sumter, South Carolina, and the Civil War begins. Union forces are defeated in Virginia at the First Battle of Bull Run (First Manassas) on July 21 and withdraw to Washington, D.C.

1862   Robert E. Lee is placed in command of the main Confederate army in Virginia in June. Lee defeats the Army of the Potomac at the Second Battle of Bull Run (Second Manassas) in Virginia on August 29–30. On September 17, Union general George B. McClellan turns back Lee's first invasion of the North at Antietam Creek near Sharpsburg, Maryland. It is the bloodiest day of the war.

1863   On January 1, President Lincoln issues the Emancipation Proclamation, freeing slaves in Southern states. Between May 1–6, Lee wins an important victory at Chancellorsville, but key Southern commander Thomas J. "Stonewall" Jackson dies from wounds. In June, Union forces hold the city of Vicksburg, Mississippi, under siege. The people of Vicksburg surrender on July 4. Lee's second invasion of the North during July 1–3 is decisively turned back at Gettysburg, Pennsylvania.

1864	General Grant is made supreme Union commander on March 9. Following a series of costly battles, on June 19 Grant successfully encircles Lee's troops in Petersburg, Virginia. A siege of the town lasts nearly a year. Union general William Sherman captures Atlanta on September 2 and begins the "March to the Sea," a campaign of destruction across Georgia and South Carolina. On November 8, Abraham Lincoln wins reelection as president.
1865	On April 2, Petersburg, Virginia, falls to the Union. Lee attempts to reach Confederate forces in North Carolina but is gradually surrounded by Union troops. Lee surrenders to Grant on April 9 at Appomattox, Virginia, ending the war. Abraham Lincoln is assassinated by John Wilkes Booth on April 14.

FURTHER READING

Chang, Ina. *Separate Battle: Women and the Civil War.* New York: Puffin, 1996.

Hakim, Joy. *War, Terrible War.* A History of US, Book 6. New York: Oxford University Press, 1994.

Haskins, Jim. *Black, Blue & Gray: African Americans in the Civil War.* New York: Simon & Schuster Books for Young Readers, 1998.

Mettger, Zak. *Reconstruction: America After the Civil War.* New York: Lodestar Books/Dutton, 1994.

Murphy, Jim. *The Journal of James Edmond Pease, a Civil War Union Solider.* A "Dear America" Book. New York: Scholastic, 1998.

INDEX

Note: **Boldface** numbers indicate illustrations.

ABOUT THE AUTHOR

AMY ALLISON, who now lives in the Los Angeles area, grew up in Washington, D.C., and Silver Springs, Maryland. Her research for this book brought back vivid memories of visits to Gettysburg and other locations where the drama of the Civil War played out. Amy's other books for Chelsea House include *Roger Williams: Founder of Rhode Island*.

PICTURE CREDITS